GRANNY'S
Nightclub Upstairs
Friday Nights
Music for All tastes
10 pm til late
Sat Nights
Music for the Masses!
10 pm til late
Room available for Private Parties

The MORNING STAR
Award Winning Food
MORNING STAR
TRADE MARK
Heineken
THE DUKE OF YORK

RUBY MURRAY
1935 - 1996
Belfast Born Singer
Performed here
1759-2009
THAT'S GUINNESS TIME
250 Remarkable Years
GUINNESS TIME AT
The Garrick
LAGER

Belfast

Belfast

A VIEW OF THE CITY

CHRIS ANDREWS

Published by
Gateway Publishing Ltd
www.gatewaysark.co.uk

ISBN 978 1 902471 14 3

Distribution by
Gateway Publishing Ltd and
Chris Andrews Publications Ltd
15 Curtis Yard
North Hinksey Lane
Oxford OX2 0LX
Tel +44(0)1865 723404
www.cap-ox.com
enquiries@cap-ox.com

Photographs by
Chris Andrews
Introductory text by
Barry Flynn
Captions by
Raymond O' Regan and
Chris Andrews
Edited by
Derek Gallop
Design by
Mike Brain at Wild Boar Design
Belfast Partner
Gareth Quinn

For personalised versions of this
book please contact
Gateway Publishing Ltd
Tel. +44 (0)1865 723404
www.gatewaysark.co.uk or
enquiries@cap-ox.com

Contents

Foreword by Professor Jim Dornan	page	7
Introduction	page	8
The City	page	17
The Docks, Shipyards and River Lagan	page	82
Queen's Quarter	page	114
The Titanic Quarter	page	134
Cathedrals, Churches and Stormont	page	160
Acknowledgements	page	180

Title page: Titanica sculpture by Rowan Gillespie outside Titanic Belfast
This page: The Albert Memorial Clock and Queen's Square

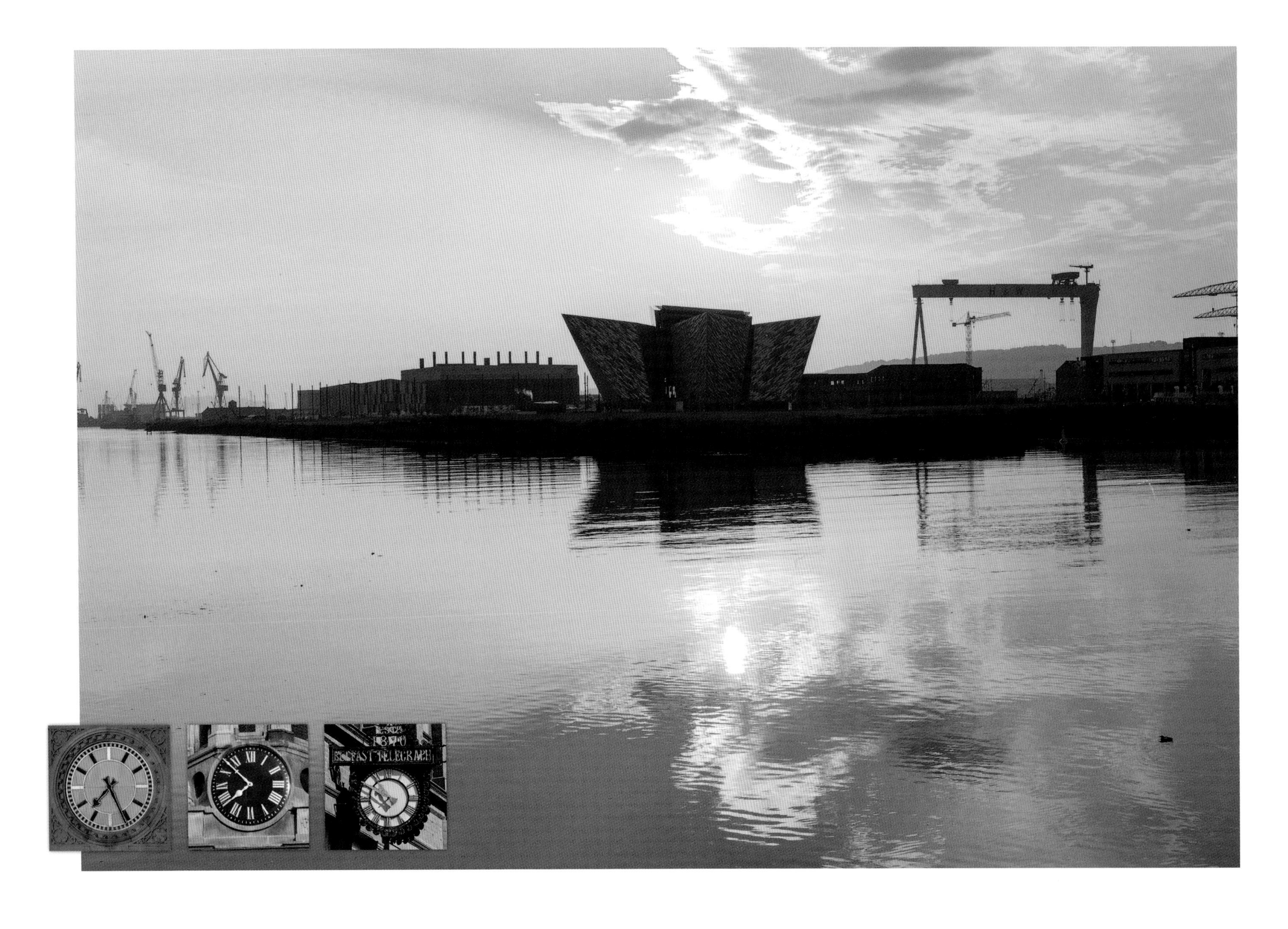

The Lagan and Queen's Island with Titanic Belfast, Harland and Wolff's site, the Titanic Film Studios and dockside cranes. Inset, some of the city's numerous clocks – a sign of a busy industrial heritage as many buildings included a timepiece to ensure punctuality by their workers

Foreword

Professor Jim Dornan MD

Belfast can be great fun, a warm and friendly city whose size is 'just right'. A Goldilocks city ... not too big, not too small. Often exciting, sometimes infuriating, invariably welcoming and never boring.

Mind you, it's no wonder we discuss the weather so much. Apart from it being a pretty safe subject, it's also true that we often experience all the seasons in one hour, never mind one day. It is a vibrant city that's always on the move. Night and day. With so many big schools, universities, commercial premises, hospitality outlets and even a golf course, all close to its centre, it truly buzzes at all hours.

The Cathedral Quarter is just the latest gem to be added to our cluster of precious stones, nestling where the Lagan meets the Lough. You can bring anyone from anywhere to Belfast and be justly proud of her blend of old and contemporary constructions, which provide everyone with good fare, entertainment, accommodation and truly interesting sights.

Many Irish and UK cities have been transformed in the past decades, and I feel that Belfast prospered by being one of the later to attempt to reinvent herself, for lots of understandable political and social reasons. But this has allowed those who are reshaping her to see the mistakes others have made, while at the same time introducing the latest in design features and materials that are in keeping with our heritage and our future. My working life has taken me round the world on frequent occasions, but this city and its population is never far from my mind.

This book has been compiled by Chris Andrews, who openly admits to having, by chance, fallen in love with both our surroundings and our people and their frequently displayed ability to enjoy the craic. His evocative photographs reveal an atmosphere and strength that is not always obvious to the passing observer. This book contains classic images portrayed in a whole new light, combined with a wealth of original insight, providing a view of the city which is always engaging and occasionally surprising.

I trust this collection will leave you with a feeling that Chris has captured our mood and our charm, a city with a proud past industrial history, a tragic fragmented recent political past, but also a place which is comfortable with itself and its people.

Belfast can just make you feel so much at home.

Belfast

Belfast is the vibrant jewel in the crown of Northern Ireland. It is a self-confident city, full of opportunity and enjoying its own unique and energetic renaissance. It is a place with a proud economic history, pulsating passion, creative culture and world-renowned friendliness. There is a lively pulse beating in the very heart of Belfast, a pulse which drives the city's rejuvenated business sector, eclectic tourist industry and burgeoning arts scene. Belfast's personality is evident within its historic buildings, famous pubs, café bars and rich cultural life. This is all manifested through a host of galleries, festivals and the now world-famous Titanic Belfast.

Small in size, Belfast is a compact metropolis with a lot to offer the businessman and tourist alike. It is a proud city encapsulated within majestic scenery, just waiting to be discovered and explored.

Belfast is enclosed between the imposing Divis and Black Mountains and the rolling Castlereagh Hills. To the north lies the spectacular sight of the historic Cave Hill, where dramatic basalt cliffs sweep down to the shore of the Lough. Formerly within the ancient lands of the O'Neill's of Clandeboye, Belfast was merely a glorified hamlet when it came into the possession of Sir Arthur Chichester in 1603. It grew in importance throughout the seventeenth and eighteenth centuries and soon eclipsed its neighbour Carrickfergus in importance as a mercantile town. Throughout the nineteenth century, rapid industrialisation transformed Belfast from a thriving town into a major city at the centre of the British Empire.

Extensive engineering projects eventually tamed the wide and meandering Lagan River where a port was established from which prosperity grew. Linen, engineering and, most famously, shipbuilding were the rocks on which Belfast's reputation and riches were founded. The industrial revolution left Belfast with a sense of civic and economic pride; it could boast amongst other things, the world's largest shipyards and linen mills; tobacco and mineral water factories; and a rope-works which dwarfed all others throughout the globe. Belfast soon eclipsed Dublin as Ireland's premier city and rivalled Glasgow, Liverpool and Manchester in size and importance.

British Airways and Aer Lingus planes at George Best Belfast City Airport

View over City Hall to Belfast Lough, the Titanic Quarter and Carrickfergus from the Hastings Grand Central Hotel

From such prosperity arose manifestations of municipal splendour which complemented the town's standing as a seat of intellectual learning, giving rise to Belfast's reputation as the 'Athens of Ireland'. Indeed, the town grew with such rapidity that its Town Hall, opened by the corporation in 1857, was soon considered inadequate and out of keeping with the ambition of Victorian Belfast. Thus began a search for a more suitable site: a search

which was accelerated by the granting of city status in 1888 and ended with the opening of the ornate city hall in Donegall Square in 1906. As a seat of local government, Belfast City Hall is truly a joy to behold. In total, the building cost just under £500,000 to build and remains the greatest testament and memorial to the prosperity of the city.

Beyond its inherent troubles, the city has come through further episodes which have threatened its continuing vibrancy. An outpost of vital strategic importance during World War II, Belfast became again a hotbed of industrial production for the war effort. It was felt that the German Luftwaffe was incapable of attacking the city. However that false sense of

Opposite: Top – St. Peter's Cathedral. Below – relaxing by the Lagan Weir
Above: St. Anne's Cathedral

security was cruelly exposed on the night of Easter Tuesday, 15 April 1941. That evening, two hundred bombers left their bases in Northern France bound for Belfast. By early morning, Belfast seemed to be totally in flames. The onslaught continued for weeks and when the attack had ended almost 1,000 lives had been lost throughout the devastated city. Many of the iconic buildings which had stood as testament to the Victorian age were destroyed. Indeed High Street was left a smouldering shell and to this day vacant land tells the tale of the Luftwaffe's visit. However, Belfast rose again from the ashes and reinvention is part of the character of the city. After the war Northern Ireland, and specifically Belfast, prospered – particularly in the 1950s and 1960s, despite the decline of its more traditional industries.

Belfast has consistently transformed itself on the world stage and has cast off long-held negative perceptions to become a place of pride and a 'must-see' on the tourist trail. Visitors today see a thriving, pulsating and creative place, which stands on the cusp of a truly golden era. It is a place that has flourished whilst looking to the future with, perhaps, a furtive glance over its shoulder at the past. It is a unique place; a legacy removed from many pre-conceived conceptions.

Yet, there is more to Belfast than just the story of a vibrant city; it is also a story of success arising from adversity. Since the mid-1990s, Belfast has thrived as an economic, cultural and tourist destination. CNN labelled Belfast one of Europe's hottest destinations in 2013. In 2006, Lonely Planet advised its readers to "get to Belfast before the rest of the world comes". The Financial Times has labelled the city as one of the Top 10 places in the world to hold a conference or a major event and the city's two airports have helped make it one of the most-visited weekend destinations in Europe.

Belfast has witnessed the fastest-growing economy of the thirty largest British cities over the past decade. It is a city that continues to grow, with evidence of economic rejuvenation to the fore amid an ever-evolving landscape. Creative industries are one of the city's many success stories. This sector is one of the fastest-growing in the United Kingdom and benefits from a young, educated and highly-motivated workforce.

Culturally, Belfast is thriving as its ever-diverse population creates a city which flourishes along with a living history and tradition. Perhaps, the greatest statement of the new, bold and confident

Opposite: The Lagan Weir and riverside.
Above: Evening view over the Westlink to the Black Mountain. The spherical sculpture at the junction with the M1 motorway, known colloquially as 'The Balls on the Falls' is more properly titled Rise

Belfast came in 2012, when Titanic Belfast opened its doors to the world. Located on former shipyard land at Queen's Island, it has been an undoubted success and typical of Belfast in that the decline of shipbuilding has acted as the catalyst for economic re-birth. Indeed the legacy of the city's shipbuilding heritage will be preserved within the Titanic Quarter where the Olympic and Titanic slipways, as well as the iconic Samson and Goliath cranes, stand proud as a testament to the past – and to the future!

Belfast is now one of the safest cities in the United Kingdom. Crime rates are low in comparison with for example Dublin, Cardiff or Rotterdam. So, relax, drink, dine and dance in one of the city's 300 pubs and restaurants; you might just be captivated.

On first impression, Belfast's greatness and grandeur may not be obvious, but scratch the surface and you will find it. It has enjoyed a re-birth to become again a vibrant and outward-looking city. It is a place driven by re-invention where character and resilience have yielded a dividend in tandem with peace. The pace of change has been considerable, but it is recognised that many challenges will still have to be faced if it is to achieve its potential to become again a world-renowned and successful city.

This book is a tribute to the people and the City of Belfast.

Opposite above: Belfast breakfast (the Ulster Fry). Below: The Botanic Garden.
Above: At the Duke of York

The Centre of Belfast,
City Hall and the Scottish
Provident Building

THE CITY

Traditional signage in the Duke of York

The Lagan Weir, Queen Elizabeth Bridge, Queen's Bridge, and developments south along the Lagan Waterfront

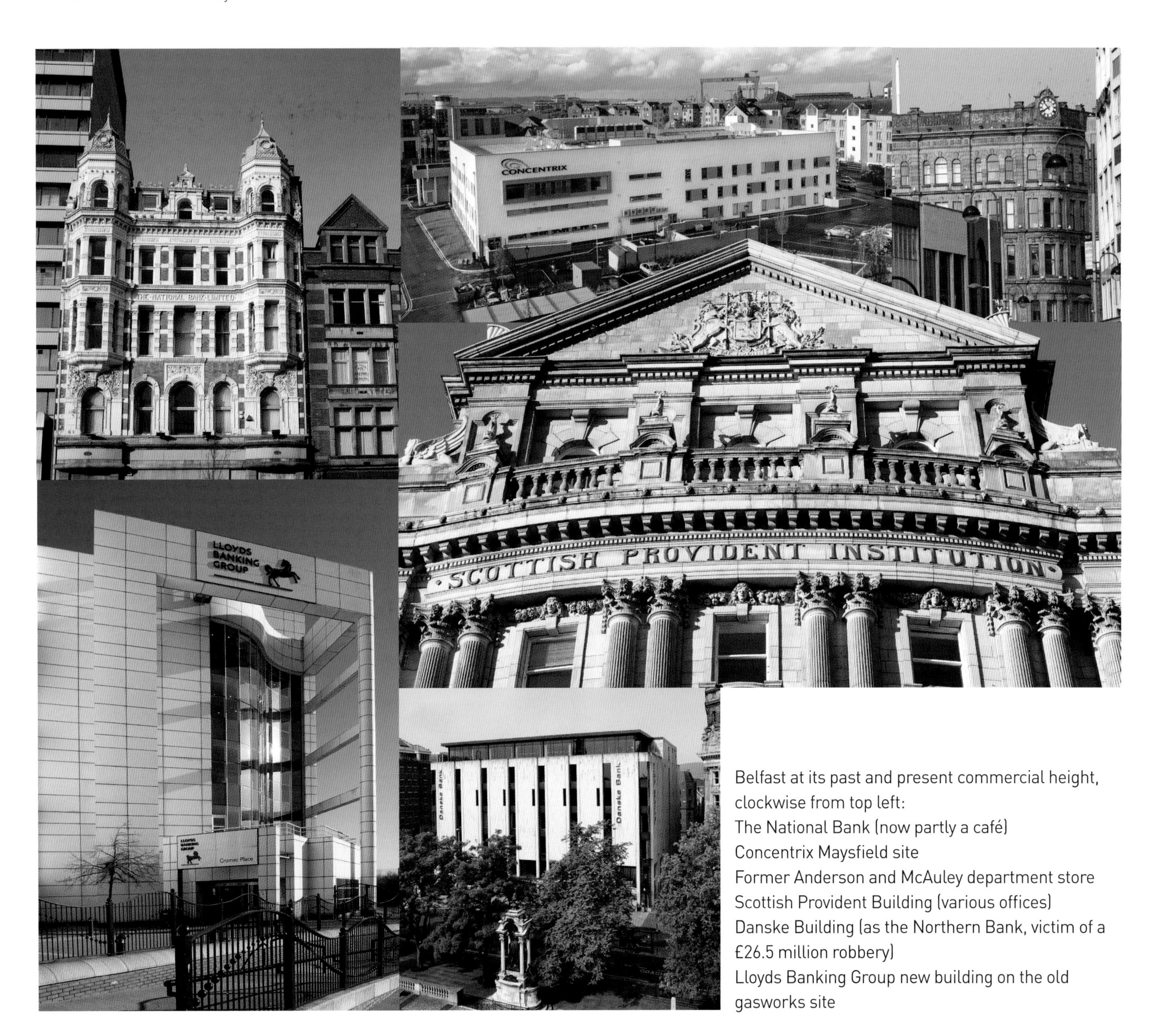

Belfast at its past and present commercial height, clockwise from top left:
The National Bank (now partly a café)
Concentrix Maysfield site
Former Anderson and McAuley department store
Scottish Provident Building (various offices)
Danske Building (as the Northern Bank, victim of a £26.5 million robbery)
Lloyds Banking Group new building on the old gasworks site

The modern Ulster Bank headquarters in Donegall Square East, a bold attempt to merge the old with the new

POTTINGER'S ENTRY.
We're
Backin'
Belfast
hotter

Opposite: A mixture of street entertainers and the striking (yellow) memorial to Sir Otto Jaffe, Belfast's first Jewish Lord Mayor.
Above: The Spirit of Belfast by Dan George, known as the 'Onion Rings', this modern sculpture dominates the centre of Arthur Square. Coloured lighting at night reflects the texture and lightness of linen while the metal itself commemorates industry, particularly shipbuilding

Seasonal shoppers

Telegraph
Telegraph
Telegraph
Telegraph
GET YOUR
COPY
HERE
TODAY

Mast sculptures along Donegall Place celebrating Harland & Wolff Shipyard's output, including the Titanic, the Olympic and the Nomadic

The Big Fish on the banks of the River Lagan shows details of Belfast's history, it was an instant tourist attraction when opened in 1999

The Albert Memorial Clock. The top of the tower leans some four feet off the perpendicular, a result of being built on wooden piles on marshy, reclaimed land around the River Farset. It is sometimes referred to as 'The Leaning Tower of Albert'. Beside the tower in Queen's Square is a noted water feature

Five minutes in Belfast: from overcast, to torrential rain, to bright sun – it's always interesting. Great Victoria Street and the Grand Opera House.

And then it rains!

The Grand Opera House of 1895, remembered as one of the regenerators of Belfast's social life during the height of the Troubles. It was not always well looked-after and, in order to save the House from imminent demolition in 1974, it was designated the first listed building in Northern Ireland

Inside the Opera House: The Shakespeare window, a programme with signatures marking the visit of General Dwight D. Eisenhower and Field Marshal Montgomery in 1945, the ornate ceiling. The latter restored in the late 1970s – the four corner paintings are original, the centre section recreated from written records after being damaged when the theatre was used as a cinema

The auditorium during a rehearsal. The detailed decorations include several circus references, possibly after the touring circus that set up on this site before the Opera House

Opposite: The Merchant Hotel in Waring Street has been fashioned from the former Ulster Bank headquarters of 1857

Bank of Ireland

Revolución de Cuba

Tesco

A few parts of the City are as yet unregenerated, the 1930s designed Bank of Ireland building is empty. However a majority of buildings, especially the many other former banks, have been given a new life and can now be seen as cafés, bars, hotels and even a supermarket

A hugely successful recent conversion has been that of the old Harland and Wolff Drawing Offices into the remarkable Titanic Hotel, situated right beside Titanic Belfast

My Belfast: Zoe Salmon

"Winning the title of Miss Northern Ireland ... meant that I got to work all over the capital and really got to know it well. I won the title in the Europa Hotel, a key feature on the Belfast skyline, and have since spent many an evening in the famous hotel at various functions. I have even abseiled down it and I can tell you that the view of Belfast from the rooftop is breathtaking!"

The Belfast skyline from the south-west soon after dawn, this is the view from the top of the Europa

Belfast life: including a tea room, and all the liveliness and characters at McHugh's, Bittles, Kelly's Cellars, Aether and Echo, the Spaniard, Monico and the MAC arts centre

My Belfast: Raymond Snoddy

"The City Hall is impressive and Queen's University is interesting but there's nothing really to beat a proper pub crawl around the historic pubs of Belfast. To do the job properly you need to set aside a day, ideally starting at Bittles Bar in Victoria Square as close to opening time as possible. Then it's round the corner to McHugh's in Queen's Square before cutting across to Kelly's Cellars in Bank Street.

After lunch, a visit to the Crown Liquor Saloon in Great Victoria Street (proprietors, the National Trust) is essential. Linger a while in its wonderful snugs before a late afternoon trip to see a film in the Odyssey for a bit of a breather. A perfect day out in Belfast can then be rounded off with a visit to the Northern Whig — not exactly an historic bar but an historic newspaper premises that have been put to an entirely appropriate use. And the really great news is that there's more than enough historic bars in Belfast still left for another day out"

More Belfast life: Murals at the Duke of York, the Morning Star, the Kitchen Bar, the Duke of York pub, the New Orpheus, and a painting inside McHugh's

The Crown

St. George's Market: There has been a Friday market on this site since 1604. The present market, built 1890–1896, is one of Belfast's oldest attractions and includes a great variety of local produce, arts, crafts and entertainment

Belfast is now well known for its great cuisine and quality local ingredients, for example a lobster thermidor at Deanes

The city and environs has a breadth of sporting clubs, events and competitions. Here (clockwise), the start of a North West 200 race, GAA - Antrim vs Laois, Ulster against the Scarlets at rugby union and a hurling match at Corrigan Park
.

CHIQUITO

Victoria Square shopping centre

The Linen Hall Library in Donegall Square North was founded in 1788 as the Belfast Reading Society. It is the oldest library in Belfast and the last subscribing library in Ireland. The library is particularly noted for its Irish and local studies collections

The City Hall, by the London architect Alfred Brumwell Thomas, opened in 1906. It is sometimes referred to as 'Wrenaissance' architecture, alluding to Wren's St. Paul's Cathedral in London. The external Portland stone contrasts with the extensive use of Greek and Italian marble within the interior

My Belfast: Barry McGuigan MBE

"I won my first Ulster Senior Title at the Ulster Hall ... The King's Hall in Balmoral was not so claustrophobic but it equalled any atmosphere that you were likely to get in any passion-filled arena in the world ... The most majestic of all these stunning buildings and the one in the forefront of my mind is, of course, the delectable Belfast City Hall, which welcomed me home after winning the World Title"

Inside City Hall:
A sculpture of the Earl of Belfast being tended to on his deathbed, chairs used by King George V and Queen Mary at the official opening of the First Northern Ireland Parliament in 1921, and a room in the visitor exhibition in the east wing

The marble staircase

In and around City Hall

A parade to the Cenotaph passes Queen Victoria's Statue. In the foreground a monument to James McGuinness, the only person from Northern Ireland to be awarded a Victoria Cross in WW II

St. Patrick's Day Parade:
Preparing a float at the Beat studios, a display leaving City Hall, Irish Dancers and more of the parade

Runners outside City Hall at the start of the Belfast half-marathon

Celebrations at Stormont and in the city to mark the 50th anniversary of Paddy Hopkirk's Monte Carlo Rally victory

ROTHMANS
ROTHMANS
1

weller

POWERED BY
COSWORTH
whittakerandwatt

JAGUAR
COVENTRY · ENGLAND

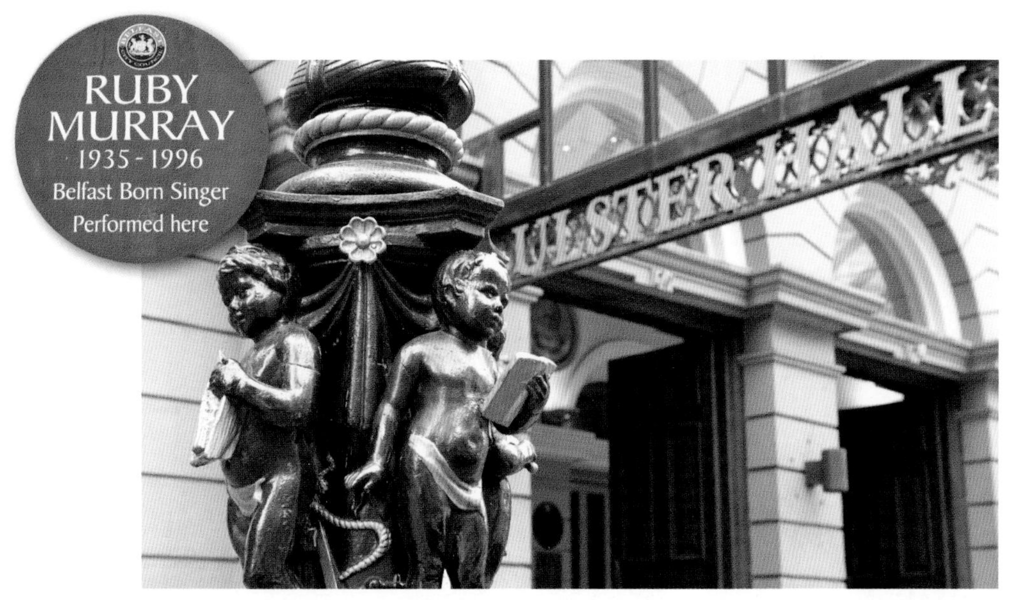

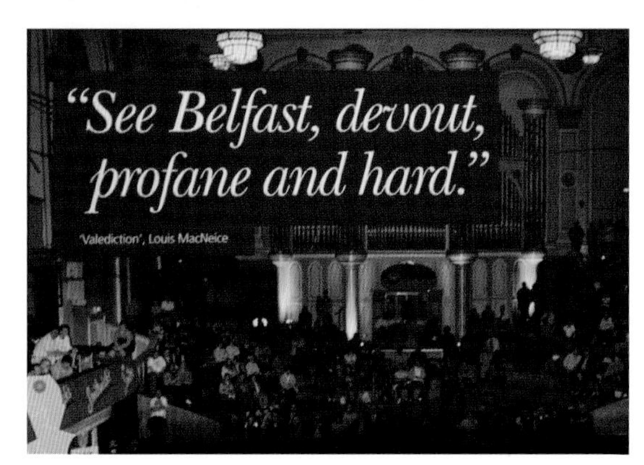

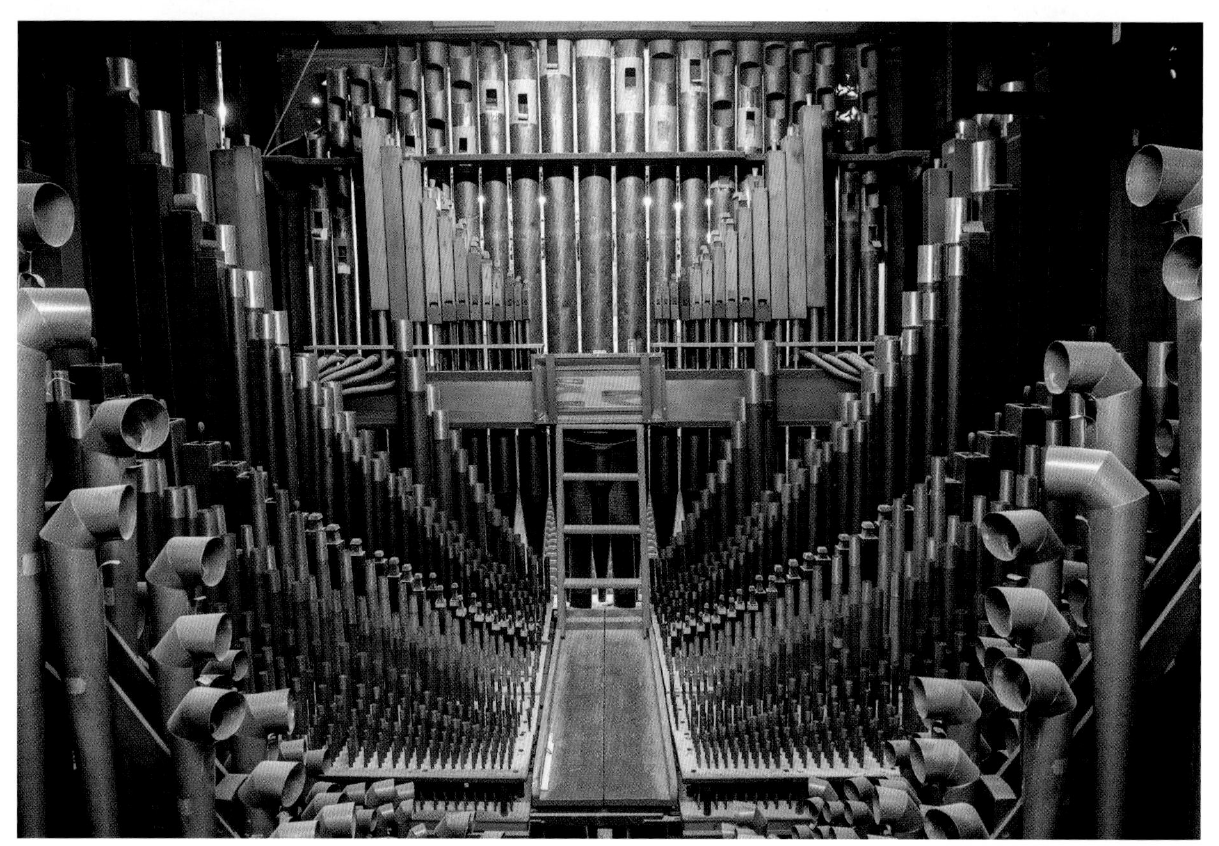

Ulster Hall with its world-famous Mullholland Grand Organ.
Designed by the architect William J. Barre and opened in 1862 the Hall has hosted many notable people and events including Charles Dickens, Lord Randolph Churchill and the Ulster Orchestra. In the Second World War it was a dance hall for American troops and since then has staged boxing matches as well as concerts, including on 5 March 1971 the first ever live performance by Led Zeppelin of their iconic song, 'Stairway to Heaven'

Ulster Hall at night after a concert

Nearby the Café Harlem and Deanes Deli Bistro

The Peace Wall and some of the famous Belfast murals, with guide.
Opposite:
Bonfires and the city scape in July

The Crumlin Road Gaol, now a tourist attraction with guided tours. The Courthouse opposite is connected by a tunnel under the road for the convicted to go straight to gaol. The Courthouse is empty and stands as a memorial to a different time

Memorials to C. S. Lewis, one of Belfast's best known writers, the life-size sculpture based on Lewis as 'The Searcher' in his work *The Chronicles of Narnia* (1950).
The mural below is a Daliesque reference at the entrance to the Duke of York pub

Street Art:
Vibrant contemporary works are on many walls throughout Belfast

The city at night can be as colourful as the murals. The Lisburn Road by Queen's University

CROMAC
PLACE

The redeveloped gasworks site; its clock tower was saved from demolition by intervention from Sir John Betjeman. By 1898, profits from the gasworks were sufficient to pay for the entire construction of the new City Hall

My Belfast: Kenneth Branagh

"As children, we walked everywhere and, where sensible, I would encourage people to do the same thing. Aside from the parks, there are so many places to explore on foot, and the obvious ones are no bad place to start. Belfast Castle, for instance, and the favourite of many; 'Napoleon's Nose' – the great Cave Hill itself"

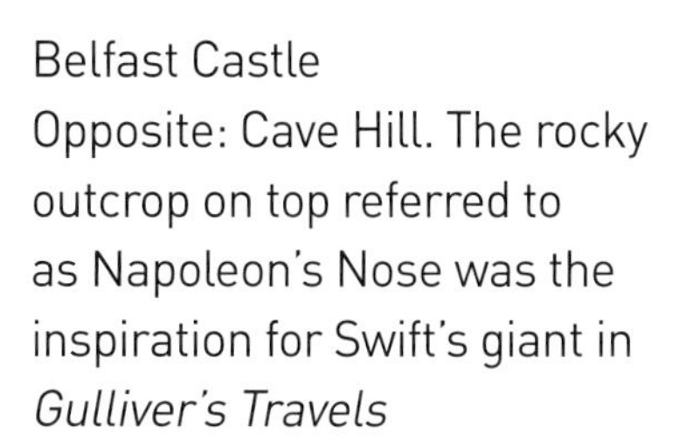

Belfast Castle
Opposite: Cave Hill. The rocky outcrop on top referred to as Napoleon's Nose was the inspiration for Swift's giant in *Gulliver's Travels*

Belfast Castle gardens and views. There are nine references to cats to be seen as well as extensive views over the Lough to the city

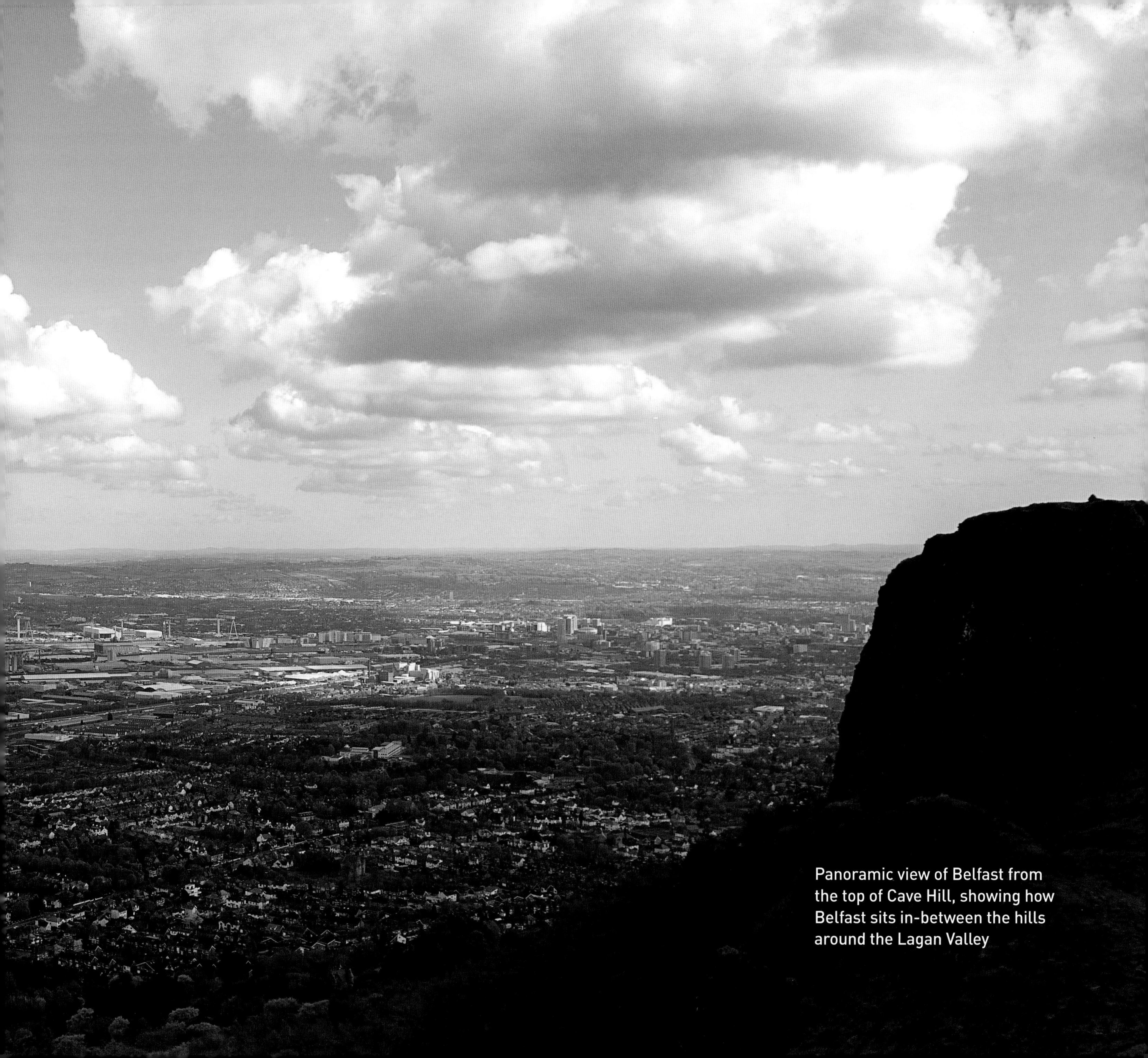

Panoramic view of Belfast from the top of Cave Hill, showing how Belfast sits in-between the hills around the Lagan Valley

Looking out over the Lough from Cave Hill. On a good day Scotland may be seen

Inland from Cave Hill towards Belfast, showing Black Mountain, Squires Hill and Divis Mountain

THE DOCKS, SHIPYARDS AND RIVER LAGAN

My Belfast: Sir James Galway ... the docks and shipyards.

"Growing up in Belfast gave me an education which set me on the road to a successful life. I don't mean Mountcollyer or Saint Paul's schools, but the city itself. ... the docks and the shipyards. We would spend hours exploring these wonderful places and being chased from them!"

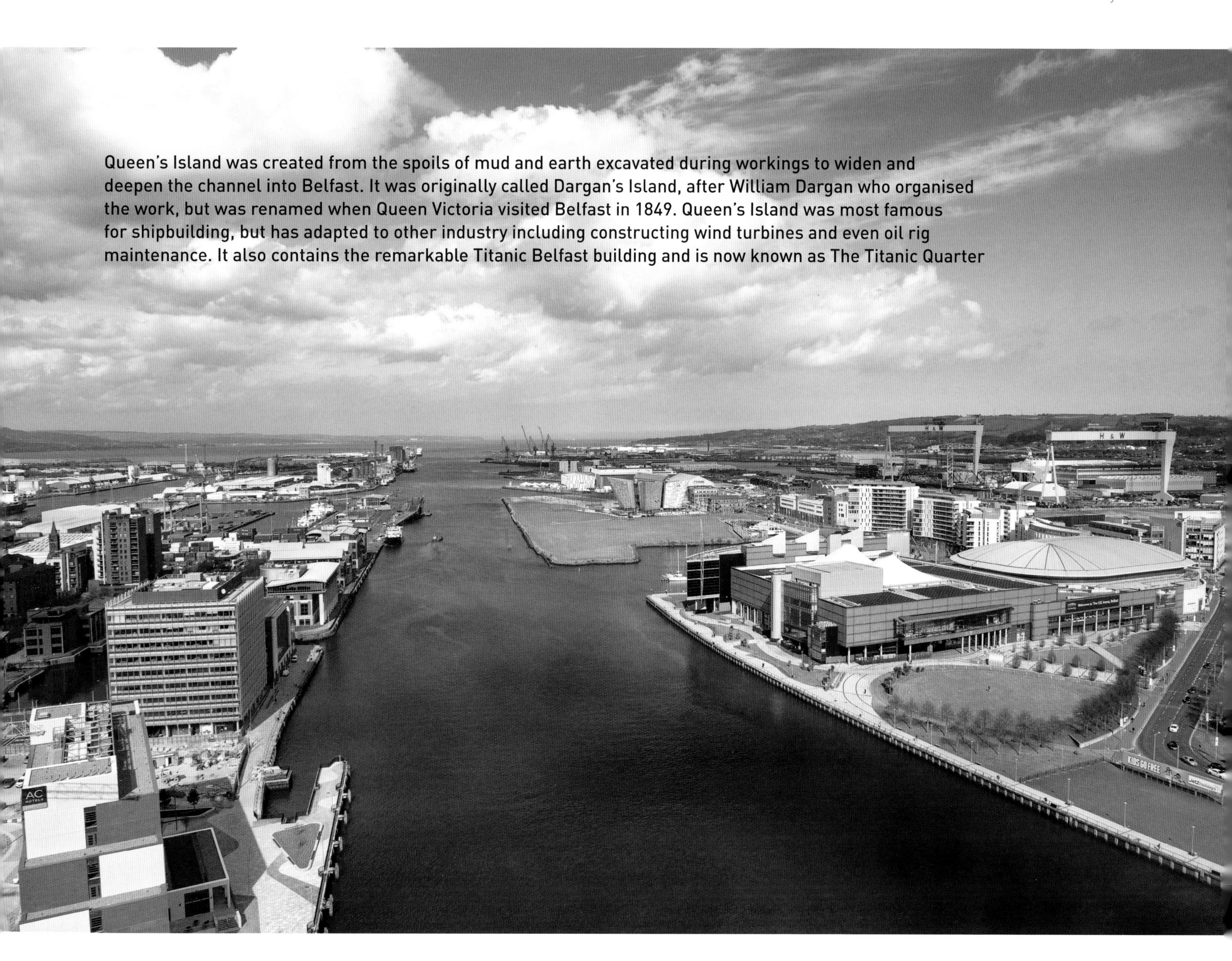

Queen's Island was created from the spoils of mud and earth excavated during workings to widen and deepen the channel into Belfast. It was originally called Dargan's Island, after William Dargan who organised the work, but was renamed when Queen Victoria visited Belfast in 1849. Queen's Island was most famous for shipbuilding, but has adapted to other industry including constructing wind turbines and even oil rig maintenance. It also contains the remarkable Titanic Belfast building and is now known as The Titanic Quarter

Wind turbine construction

A cargo crane, apartment blocks and the Odyssey Trust buildings.
Opposite: Sunrise over Titanic Belfast and Queen's Island

NORSE CHARTERS
SURVEY

The Harbour Office has been the headquarters of the Belfast Harbour Commissioners since 1847, the style of architecture based on that of an Italian palazzo

Inside the building there is a display featuring the Edwardian mahogany table and Queen Anne-style chairs that were intended for the private quarters of the Titanic's captain, Edward John Smith. However, because of a late delivery, they never reached their destination. Taking into account this history, the Antiques Roadshow found them literally priceless

A new permanent exhibition in the Harbour Office entitled 'A Port that Built A City', to celebrate 400 years of Belfast's maritime history, was recently opened, including this spectacular new stained glass panel (right) commissioned from the artist Ann Smith

Opposite:
Belfast's Harbour Commissioners Office and the city over the Abercorn Basin

The Clarendon Graving Docks were used to work on ships' hulls once the gates had closed and the water pumped out. The first dock was finished in 1800 by William Ritchie, a Scot credited with starting shipbuilding in Belfast. The long low building was the pumphouse and workshop

Black Guillemots, a Black-headed Gull and a Common Tern around the Lagan Weir

The Lagan below the weir, Custom House in the centre is where the novelist Anthony Trollope worked as a surveyor from 1853. He wrote *'The Warden'* and much else of the *'Barsetshire Chronicles'* while living in the City. The Obel Tower on the right became the tallest building in Northern Ireland on completion in 2010

'Harmony', or the Beacon of Hope statue on Thanksgiving Square

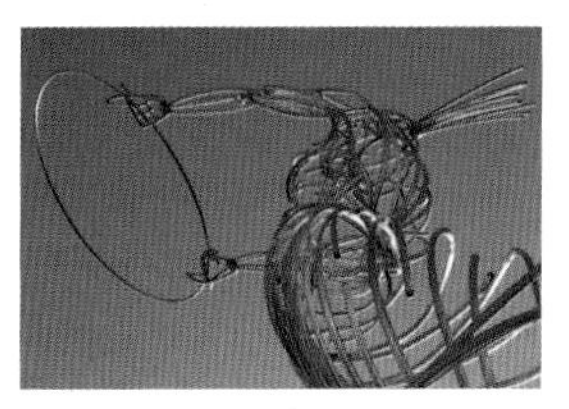

Sculpture by the Belfast Waterfront celebrating the city's brewing history. At one time Belfast produced 3,000,000 gallons of whiskey each year – 60% of Ireland's total output, as well as a good quantity of beer

Views and buildings on the redeveloped quayside around the Belfast Waterfront and Thanksgiving Square

MUSEUM
OPEN

Dawn at the Lagan Weir

Bringing Life to The Lagan
Bringing Life to The Lagan

The MV Confiance is a former cargo barge, now fully renovated to house a museum, a multi-use performance space and a café

Belfast Waterfront, opened in 1997, is an award-winning conference, arts and entertainment centre

The Ulster Orchestra and the Belfast Philharmonic Choir at rehearsal in the Belfast Waterfront

Lagan quayside, looking back to the City

The Belfast Waterfront, the MV Confiance and offices just before dawn. Early birds make faint blurred shapes in the sky

RSM McClure Watters

Rail bridge over the Lagan

Harland and Wolff's iconic cranes at sunrise

St. George's Harbour apartments and the Albert Bridge

A chimney stands as sole reminder of the former Sirocco Works where at one time most of the world's tea drying machinery was produced. Later diversifying into ventilation systems, the first air conditioning system was developed here and the Royal Victoria Hospital in Belfast was the first building in the world to have it fitted

My Belfast: Dame Mary Peters

"... to this day I enjoy visiting the Lagan Towpath, ... (and walk along to) the rose gardens ..."

Old Lock Bridge at Ormeau Embankment

Reflections in the windows and the new Allstate building on the banks of the Lagan. Opposite: a view back to the city from the towpath

H & W

QUEEN'S QUARTER

Belfast Botanic Gardens opened in 1828 as the 'Private Royal Belfast Botanical Gardens', becoming a public park in 1895. It has one of the earliest examples of a curvilinear cast iron glasshouse in the world

The Palm House was designed by Charles Lanyon and built by Dubliner Richard Turner in 1830–52. It predates both Glassnevin and Kew Gardens Glass Houses

Entertainer Bruce Forsyth's grandfather was curator of the Royal Botanic Gardens in 1869

Plants and visitors in the Botanic Gardens

The Tropical Ravine House opened in 1889. A sunken ravine runs the length of the building with many interesting plants, including a giant cycad. This sort of vegetation might have hidden Triceratops, but the skeleton opposite is in the Ulster Museum, which backs onto the building and the Botanic Gardens

st and the
nd World War

Tree-lined footpaths through the Botanic Gardens lead to the Ulster Museum and Queen's University.

The Ulster Museum is home to a rich collection of art, history and natural sciences. The revitalised museum also tells the story of the people of the north of Ireland from earliest times to the present day

The Museum hosts many events, including this one for the BBC's 'MacNeice Week' commemorating the Belfast-born poet. Louis Mac Neice (1907–1963) was a contemporary of W. H. Auden and Stephen Spender at Oxford and his work is a considerable influence on new generations of Northern Irish poets

Newsreader Tara Mills and the BBC Newsline studio

My Belfast: Nick Ross

"Belfast is a hugely friendly city ... and along with some of the best watering holes in the world it now has seriously fine restaurants, great cultural centres and a bustling nightlife ...

The fabric of the city is incomparably improved since I first arrived there – but the place that for me became home, around Queen's University, is more or less unchanged. The whole campus district around University Road, College Green and University Square still has a classic, slightly battered, academic elegance"

Queen's University Quadrangle

The new McClay Library at the University

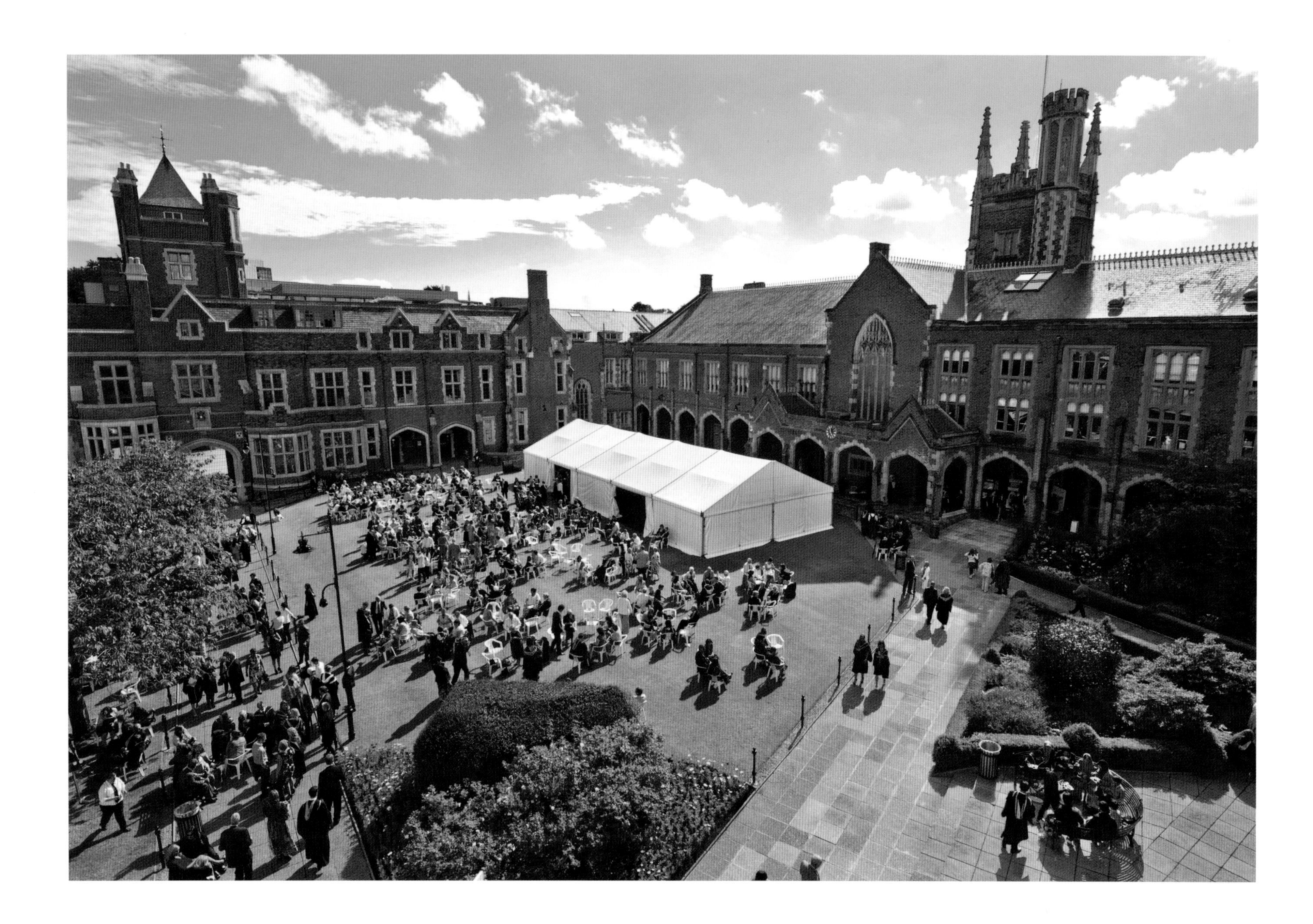

Queen's University was opened as Queen's College in 1849, and was one of three non-denominational colleges throughout Ireland. The name was changed to Queen's University in 1908. Pictured above is the Graduation Garden Party

The Lanyon Building

The great stained glass window in Queen's entrance hall is a memorial to all of those from the University who died in both World Wars. It was designed in 1939 by J E Nuttgens

to receive the
instruction of
wisdom, jus-
tice &
subtilty
to the simple
to the young
man knowledge & dis
cretion.
WISDOM
ALMA MATER
TEMPERANCE
JUSTICE
UNIVERSITY

Belfast is responsible for many advances in medical knowledge, including in trauma surgery, obstetrics and the development of the portable defibrillator. Work in the last few years here has even included research into Viagra and its effects!

Belfast City Hospital dominates the skyline along the Lisburn Road (it is one of the tallest buildings in Northern Ireland) and there are three other major hospitals in the city. Recently a number of private healthcare providers, including the 3fivetwo Group, have evolved to further develop medical advances and to help fulfil the needs of the population

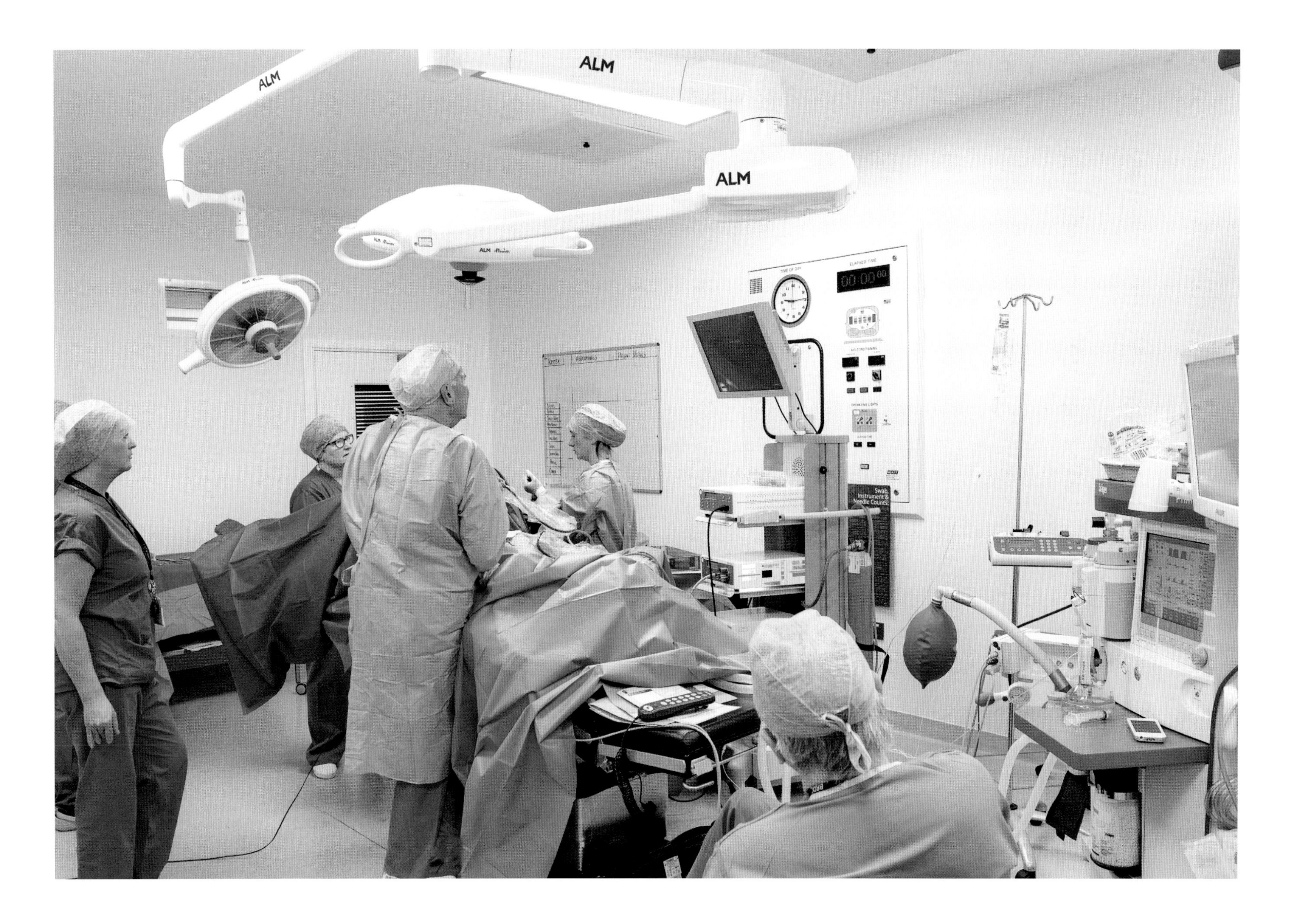

Professor James Dornan operating in Kingsbridge Private Hospital

THE TITANIC QUARTER

Redevelopment of the former docks and shipyard including Titanic Belfast and the Titanic Film Studios, the latter where Game of Thrones is filmed

Spring

Titanic Belfast and the lough. The building itself represents the shape of ships' hulls

The restored slipway at the back of Titanic Belfast down which Titanic was launched.
To the left are the old Harland and Wolff drawing offices, now the Titanic Hotel

Celebrations inside Titanic Belfast including an interview on the Titanic Grand Staircase replica

Inside the ground floor of Titanic Belfast

The former drawing offices, now the Titanic Hotel, with Titanic Belfast and Cave Hill from corner of the old Harland and Wolff factory site

Titanic Studios, formerly the Harland and Wolff paint hall, and one of the many sets built for the series Game of Thrones that is filmed in the building

The two cranes are called Samson and Goliath

A tour by boat shows the whole Titanic and dockland waterways

Belfast's Urban Sports Park T13 is set in a former shipbuilding warehouse beside the working area of Harland and Wolff. T13 offers everything from BMX (demonstrated here by Matt, defying gravity) to skateboarding, urban art to DJ sessions.
The oil rig came from Brazil for refit at the city's dockyard

BLACKFORD DOLPHIN

The Titanic Quarter in winter

Goliath reflected

The SS Nomadic appropriately berthed within sight of Titanic Belfast. Nomadic was one of the last White Star ships to be built by Harland and Wolff and is the only remaining White Star Line ship in the world

The interior of the Nomadic. In her day she was used to transfer the first and second class passengers onto the Olympic and Titanic liners at Cherbourg. The third class passengers used the Traffic, a smaller, much less luxurious vessel

Inside and outside of the Nomadic, now beautifully restored after returning from France

NOMADIC
CHERBOURG

HMS Caroline moored in the Titanic Quarter. She was built by Cammell Laird in time for the outbreak of the Great War. Launched and commissioned in 1914, she joined the Grand Fleet at Scapa Flow. She came to Belfast in 1924 and was used as the headquarters of the Royal Naval Volunteer Reserve, and is now restored as a museum

HMS Caroline was the second-oldest commissioned ship in the Royal Navy until her decommissioning in 2011 – HMS Victory is the first. She is also the last surviving vessel of any nation which fought at the Battle of Jutland and one of only three surviving Royal Navy warships from the First World War. (Shown here before restoration)

The Caroline's engine room, she was driven by steam turbines and was one of the fastest ships of her time

Officer's accommodation

The triple wooden wheel below decks which was connected directly to the rudder, it was manned whenever the ship was manoeuvring in a tight space in case of any failure of the power steering

The ship's crew were fed from this tiny galley with a cast iron range for cooking

The Thompson Dry Dock where Titanic sat before her first, and last voyage. A replica of Titanic's bow can be seen on the dock side

The Pump House and dry dock area

CATHEDRALS, CHURCHES AND STORMONT

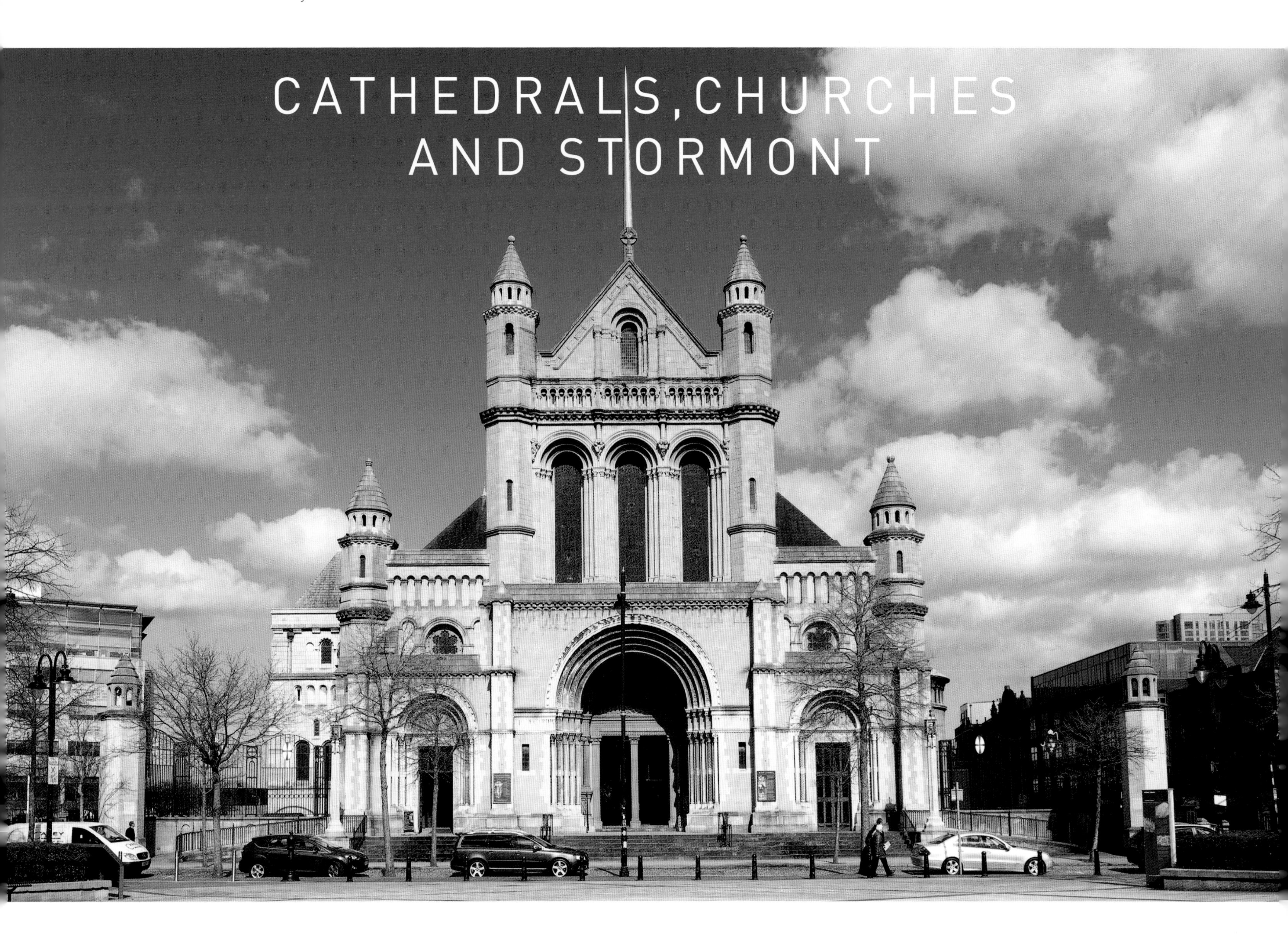

St. Anne's Cathedral

The cathedral was begun in 1896, though not finally completed until 2007 when the striking metal spine was installed

The memorial lectern (left) was presented by the Officers of the 36th (Ulster) Division, containing eight volumes with the names of those Irish killed serving in the First World War

St. Peter's Cathedral opened in 1866, though the magnificent twin spires were not added until 1886. A recent renovation has enhanced its remarkable Gothic interior

The Church of the Most Holy Redeemer at Clonard Monastery

St. George's Church was built in 1816 but there were two previous churches on this site dating as far back as medieval times – one was the Little Church of the Ford and the other the early 17th century Corporation Church

Saint Malachy's.
The castle-like exterior and studded Tudor-style door of St. Malachy's opens onto an incredible interior with a ceiling like an inside-out wedding cake. In 1868, the largest bell turret in Belfast was added to the church. It was taken away shortly afterwards, due to complaints that its deafening noise interfered with the maturing of the whiskey in Dunville's nearby distillery!

The Church is regarded as one of the finest examples of Tudor Revival churches in Ireland.
A £3.5 million restoration project was completed in 2009

The First Presbyterian Church has always been a very liberal church since the First Session of Presbyterianism Belfast in 1644. The present church is the third on this site in Rosemary Street and dates back to 1783. It hosts popular lunchtime concerts in the summer. The painting is of the Reverend McBride who refused to sign the *Notice of Adjuration* and had to escape the city. The Sovereign (Mayor) of the time stabbed the portrait when he discovered that the Reverend McBride had fled to Scotland

Parliament Buildings at Stormont opened in 1932 and seats the Northern Ireland Assembly. The original design was based on the State Capital Building in Washington DC, but had to be scaled back due to lack of finance. The original name of the estate was Storm Mount, but over the years referred to as Stormont

My Belfast: Maxine Mawhinney

"My grandfather had a vintage car and we would go driving on a Sunday afternoon. We would arrive in grand style at the gates of Stormont, he in his driving hat and me in my best frock. Then there was the walk up the 'Royal Mile', the sweeping driveway to the front steps. It was probably the first measurement I ever truly understood after walking it a few times on very young legs.

Belfast for me is familiar and comfortable and yet never fails to surprise and excite. There is an energy and enthusiasm rarely matched anywhere else I have been in the world. 'No problem' is the most used phrase you will hear – nothing is ever any trouble"

The Great Hall is the grand entrance of the Parliament Buildings

The vista looking back down the hill at Stormont, dominated by the statue of Lord Carson, who famously led Ulster Protestants against Home Rule in the early part of the 20th century. He was a barrister who also defended the Marquess of Queensberry against Oscar Wilde's libel charge

The Lough at Holywood, looking back towards the city

Belfast at dusk

Leaving Belfast

'Napoleon's Nose', the inspiration for Gulliver's giant

My Belfast: Simon Callow CBE

"I came back as soon as I could, at the height of the bombing, and again and again over the years, and watched its face change almost out of recognition till it finally stepped out of the shadow of both Dublin and London and became a great European city in its own right, almost a beauty. But if its face has changed, its identity hasn't – it's still witty, capricious, cussed, tenacious and defiant, which is of course why one still keeps coming back"

Acknowledgements:

This book has been made with support of the businesses and people of Belfast and in particular:

The 3fivetwo Group
www.3fivetwo.com

*Thanks to Belfast City Council for permission to quote from its
leaflet ***My Belfast*** and for use of the Belfast Coat of Arms

The Office of The Lord Mayor
www.belfastcity.gov.uk

Visit Belfast
www.visit-Belfast.com

Gareth Quinn, our Belfast partner,
www.linkedin.com/in/garethquinn

Callow Event Management
www.callowevents.co.uk

Titanic Quarter
www.titanicquarter.com

Titanic Belfast
www.titanicbelfast.com

Rickety Bridge Winery
www.ricketybridgewinery.com

BelfastHarbour
www.belfast-harbour.co.uk

Queen's University Belfast
www.qub.ac.uk

Deanes Restaurants
www.michaeldeane.co.uk

Goldblatt McGuigan
www.goldblattmcguigan.com

And in addition, all those pictured and involved who have been so helpful:

The Ulster Hall, Ulster Rugby, John Mcilwaine for the GAA/Hurling photos, the Europa Hotel staff, Savills (NI) Limited, Belfast's pubs, restaurants, cafés and bars, Waterstones, Belfast's street performers and artists, Miss Northern Ireland, Belfast Botanic Gardens, Belfast Castle, the Linen Hall Library, Queen's University Belfast, the Crumlin Road Gaol, Titanic Boat Tours, Titanic Hotel, (pic of Hull drawing office with naval architects by Robert John Welch, (18591936) © National Museums NICollection Ulster Folk & Transport Museum), HMS Caroline, BBC Northern Ireland, Game of Thrones, T13, Ginger Andrews (photo p32), Professor Jim and Dr Samina Dornan, Barry Bingham at Offshore Investment, Sam Goldblatt, Leo Callow, Mark Marais, Karin Jeffrey, Willie Jack at Commercial Court Inns Ltd

The Belfast Daily Mercury
WOOLWORTH'S
RUBY
MURRAY
1935-1996
Belfast Born Singer
Performed here
BELFAST TELEGRAPH
1759-2009
THAT'S
GUINNESS
TIME
250
Remarkable Years
GUINNESS TIME AT
The Garrick
HARP
LAGER
THE DUKE OF